Become a Centennial Junior Ranger

Although the National Park Service takes care of these special places, we all own them together – that means you, too! And, just like you help care for your home or pets (think chores), we need your help to care for our national parks. Imagine what parks would be like in another 100 years if no one helped protect them. You can start by completing each activity below to become an official Centennial Junior Ranger!

○ Attend a ranger led activity or watch a film in a park or one of the many Youtube videos at youtube.com/user/NationalParkService

　　Name of program: _____
　　Something that I learned: _____
　　_____

○ Go for a hike on a national park trail, a trail near your home or visit an exhibit at a park visitor center.

　　Name of trail or exhibit: _____

○ Complete at least the following number of activities in this book:

　　Ages 6 and under: 5 activities
　　Ages 7-10: 7 activities
　　Ages 11 and older: 10 activities

○ Care for this park and others by following the park rules and teaching others to do the same.

Bring your completed booklet to any national park visitor center to receive your official Junior Ranger Centennial Badge! You can also send your completed booklet to the National Park Service, National Junior Ranger Program Coordinator, 1201 Eye Street NW, 8th Floor, Washington, DC 20005. Completed booklets will be returned so make sure to include your address.

Illustrations Copyright 2015
Jennifer Johnson Hay

National Park Service Symbols

Each element of this symbol represents something that is protected by the National Park Service. Use the words on the right and below to fill in the blanks.

The _____ represents wildlife.

The _____ represents plants.

The _____ represents geology.

The _____ represents natural resources such as water and air.

The _____ represents the history of our country.

Arrowhead

National Park Service

Mountain

Bison

Tree

Lake

Let's start today to help make sure the National Parks are in great shape 100 years from now. Draw your own symbols on the arrowhead to the left showing things that you think need to be protected.

How do you know you are in a place that is cared for by the National Park Service?

_____

_____

How many arrowheads can you find as you explore the park today? _____

For sale by the Superintendent of Documents, U.S. Government Publishing Office
Internet: bookstore.gpo.gov Phone: toll free (866) 512-1800; DC area (202) 512-1800
Fax: (202) 512-2104 Mail: Stop IDCC, Washington, DC 20402-0001

ISBN 978-0-16-093239-7

Jammin' Journal

Park rangers write their observations and park experiences in journals. What has inspired the hidden author in you during your visit to a park?

Date:

Location:

Weather Observation: temperature, precipitation and cloud cover:

An interesting thing I learned today is:

My favorite part of the park is:

I am happy this place was saved because:

Become a Modern Day John Muir!

Sometimes a big difference can be made by just one person or a small group of people. John Muir helped preserve Yosemite and Sequoia National Parks, and many more people throughout history have worked hard to convince others that a place is special enough to be protected and preserved. Think of a place that is special to you. Now imagine that someone else wanted to build something over it, or tear it down. How would you convince them it was worth saving? Here are a few reasons why people might create a new park. Mark the things that apply to your special place and explain why you marked them in the space below.

- ○ It has value in teaching people about science, preservation or our nation's history.
- ○ It brings outdoor recreation to residents of our cities.
- ○ It offers places for people to relax and heal.
- ○ It tells the story of a national hero or other person who helped make America great.
- ○ It helps protect native cultures.

I marked these things because: _____

_____

There are two ways that an area can become part of the National Park System:

1. For an area to become a national park, more than half of the members of Congress need to vote yes.

2. Using a special power called the Antiquities Act, presidents can designate and protect areas such as national monuments and memorials.

Think of your special place. What would you say to Congress to convince at least half of them that it is worth saving?

_____

_____

_____

Congratulations! Congress has decided to make your special place a new national park! Write its name on the sign. Now draw a picture of it in the white space and tell us why it's so special.

Past and Present Native Cultures

Before the United States became a country and long before National Parks were established, there were many people who lived on this land. You might know them as American Indians, Alaska Natives or Hawaiians. Although they may not live in the park you are visiting now, you can figure out what type of Native American might have been here.

Think way back, way before the United States was formed. Who lived here? What type of native cultures lived where you are today? Look at the map and find where you are in the country.

What type of native people were from here?
_____

Go outside and find a place on the grass or dirt, look around you, what do you see?
_____
_____
_____

What would these people use to make their homes?
_____
_____
_____

What would they have hunted to eat?
_____
_____

What plants would they have eaten?
_____
_____

What is the weather like?
_____

Do you think they would have lived here year round?
_____

When the United States became a country many of the Native Americans were moved far from their homes so that cities and farms could be made. Have you ever had to leave your home and community? America still has many native peoples, some may even live in your neighborhood. Today you can learn about and honor native people by visiting national parks that teach about their life-ways and cultures.

National Park Crossword

Use the clues below and those throughout the book to solve the crossword.

Across
5. The animal that represents wildlife in the NPS
8. The US President's program to get kid every 4th grade student in a park
9. Folded papers that help you find places.
10. A promise to teach others about the National Park Service
11. The book that rangers take notes in about their experiences
13. The type of park that is on the coastlines of America

Down
1. The symbol of the National Park Service
2. The places that protect the stories and places of history
3. Those that lived here before National Parks were established
4. Who owns the National Parks?
6. What is the word for a 100 year anniversary?
7. The person that can use the Antiquities Act to make a National Monument
12. The person who helped to save Yosemite and Sequoia national parks

Answers: 1. arrowhead 2. historic sites 3. native people 4. us citizens 5. bison 6. centennial 7. president 8. every kid in a park 9. maps 10. pledge 11. journal 12. John Muir 13. seashore

My Space – Your Space

Have you had a great visit? Are there things you saw, learned or did that you are excited to share with others? Then go for it! Help spread the word about our wonderful national parks so others will want to visit and help care for them too.

Use this page to tell us what you liked about your visit. Do you have a favorite photo you took? Paste it here. Share what you've discovered on your favorite social media site or at http://findyourpark.com/share Always ask a parent before sharing photos and information on the internet.

What hashtags might you use? For example: #Ilovenationalparks, #hike, #bisonarecool, #wishyouwerehere

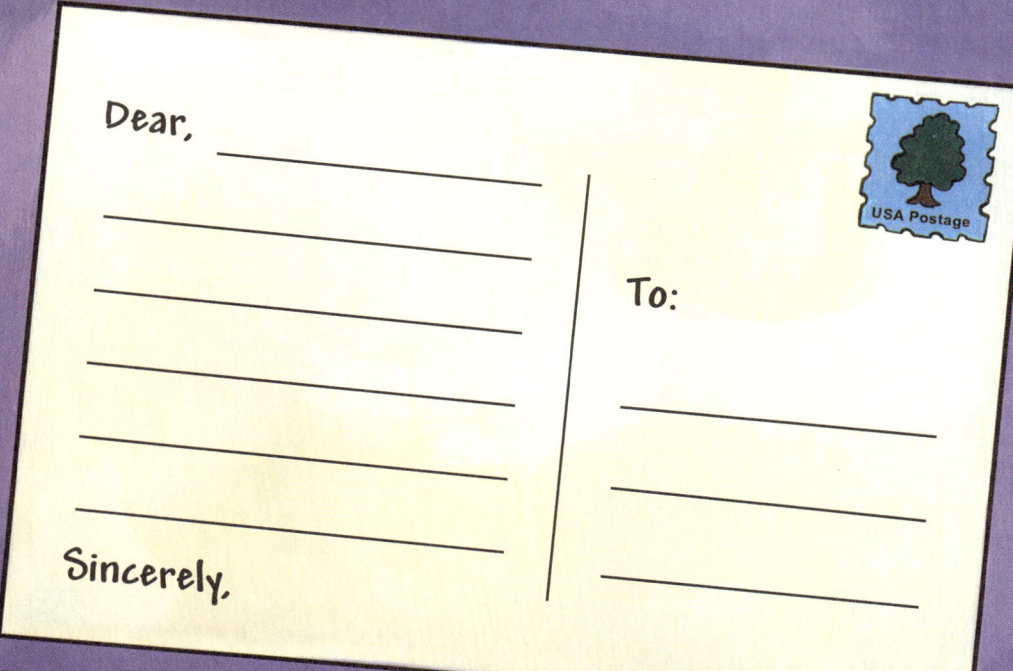

1872 - Yellowstone is first area in the world to be designated a national park

1872

1900

1901- 1909 President Theodore Roosevelt protec[ts] the Grand Canyo[n] and other parks and monument[s]

Timelines tell a story and help us understand history. They also tell us what happened when and how much time went by between events. Follow the timeline to see examples of how the National Park System has evolved since 1872. Complete the drawing activities and those below to learn more about some of these places.

- You too are a part of this history. Mark your birthday on the timeline.

- Think about two special accomplishments in your life. Add those dates to the timeline.

- Find one significant date from the park that you are visiting and add that to the time line.

1954-75 Vietnam War

1950 – Yearly visitation to national parks reaches 32 million a year

1950

1964 – Wilderness Act is signed into law

1972 – More city (urban) parks are added to the national park system

1951- National Park Service develops the first version of the arrowhead logo

1950-53 Korean Wa[r]

1975

Draw the arrowhead logo

1978 – Female rangers allowed to wear same uniform as male rangers

1981 – Mammoth Cave, the world's longest cave system, becomes a World Heritage Site

1980 – Largest national park (Wrangell-St. Elias National Park and Preserve) is established

1994 – A park celebrating the origins and evolution of jazz is created (New Orleans Jazz National Historic Park)

Write Yourself into National Park Service History!

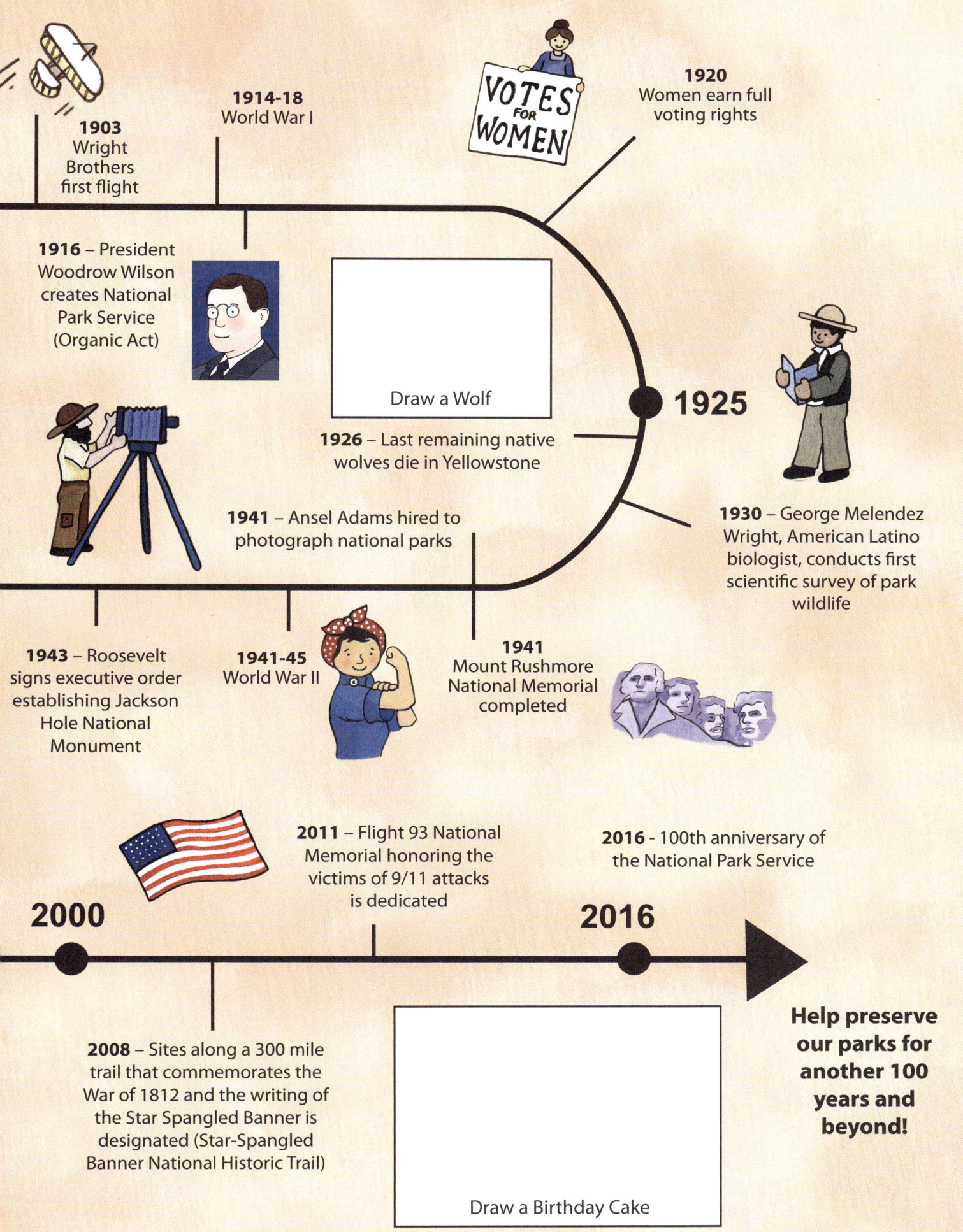

Rappin' with a Ranger

Have you heard the expression, "It takes all kinds?" Well, when it comes to running a national park – it's true. Not all park service employees are out chatting up the visitors or hanging with the bears! There are law enforcement rangers, architects, historians, computer specialists, accountants. But all of them hope to make our parks better for the future. Find a park ranger, a volunteer, or a staff member and ask them these questions about their job.

What type of work do you do? _____

What is your favorite part of your job? _____

_____

_____

Why did you decide to work (or volunteer) for the National Park Service? _____

_____

How are you helping to make your park better for the future? _____

_____

Draw a picture of you or your new ranger friend.
Don't forget your smile and your badge.

The Next Generation of Park Caregivers

Our parks will always need people to care for, protect, and preserve our national parks. You can help!

What type of National Park Service employee or volunteer would you like to be?

_____

_____

_____

Why? _____

_____

_____

Wrangell-St. Elias in Alaska is the largest park, covering 13.2 million acres, and has a glacier as big as the state of Rhode Island.

If you could hold your breath that long, it would take you about an hour to swim to the bottom of the deepest lake in the country - Crater Lake, found in Crater Lake National Park.

Complete the following map activities:

Put a square around the state where you live.

Circle three national parks you have visited and write them on the lines below. If you can't find the names on the map, write them in.

_____

_____

_____

Draw a star on the parks that you would most like to visit.

In the box below, draw something from the park you are visiting and a line to its location on the map.

The nation's deepest cave is 1,593 feet deep in New Mexico at Carlsbad Caverns National Park.

More than 400,000 people volunteer in national parks.

The President is Calling You

Like the kids in your school, national parks come in all shapes and sizes. In addition to famous ones like Yellowstone National Park, there are monuments, historic homes, native sites, seashores and scenic trails. Even the home of the US President – the White House - is a national park.

One thing all of these sites have in common is that they want kids to explore them. In fact, the President is offering every fourth grader a free pass to a park! Get the scoop at www.everykidinapark.gov

The smallest park is Thaddeus Kosciuszko National Memorial in Pennsylvania, is .002 acres - no bigger than your typical classroom.

Casa Grande ("Great House") Ruins in Arizona is the site of one of the largest prehistoric structures ever built in North America.

Protecting Special Places

Our parks and our earth need you! Caring for our national parks and our earth takes everyone. Use the sign language symbols in the box to break the code and find out some of the things that you can do to help.

- _ _ _ _ _ _ _ (RECYCLE)
- Use less _ _ _ _ (WATER)
- Pick up _ _ _ _ _ _ and put in trash _ _ _ (LITTER) (CAN)
- Use a _ _ _ _ _ _ _ _ _ water bottle (REUSABLE)
- _ _ _ _ & _ _ _ _ when possible (WALK) (BIKE)
- _ _ _ _ _ _ _ lights when not in use (TURN OFF)

Junior Ranger Centennial Pledge

As a Junior Ranger, I promise to teach others about what I learned today, explore other parks and historic sites, and help preserve and protect these places so future generations can enjoy them for the next 100 years and beyond.